The Friends of the
Western Buddhist Order

An Introduction

Dharmachari Vessantara

Windhorse Publications

Published by
Windhorse Publications
Unit 1-316 The Custard Factory
Birmingham, B9 3AA

© Windhorse Publications 1996

Printed by F. Crowe & Sons Ltd
11 Concorde Road
Norwich NR6 6BJ

Cover design by Graham Parker
The cover shows the main Buddha image
at the London Buddhist Centre

Photo credits:
page 4 © Clear Vision Trust Picture Archive
pages 10 and 31 courtesy of Dhammarati
page 13, (top) courtesy of Gonzalo Pereira, *(bottom):* courtesy of Vidyamala
back cover (top to bottom): courtesy of Jan Parker; © Clear Vision Trust Picture
Archive; courtesy of Graham Parker; © Clear Vision Trust Picture Archive;
courtesy of Vidyavati

British Library Cataloguing in Publication Data
A catalogue record for this book is available from the British Library

ISBN 1 899579 22 2

Contents

A Buddha image at the London Buddhist Centre

Introduction

The Buddha never drove a car. He never drank Coca-Cola. He never worried about nuclear proliferation. And yet, 2,500 years after his death, his teaching is being found relevant by millions of people in the modern world. In fact, Buddhism is one of the fastest growing spiritual traditions in the West.

Since 1967 the Friends of the Western Buddhist Order (FWBO) has been introducing the teaching and practice of Buddhism in a way that is particularly suited to people living in modern, industrialized society. This booklet will explain what the FWBO is about, and what it has to offer.

Buddhism in a nutshell

The FWBO is the Friends of the Western *Buddhist* Order. It is a movement that derives its inspiration from the Buddha. Buddhism is a tradition of teaching and practice that helps people to unfold the inner riches of love, wisdom, and energy that lie within us all. It is a treasure-house of guidance and help for those who wish to develop ever higher levels of being and consciousness. It is a path which culminates in Enlightenment, or Buddhahood.

The word 'Buddha' means 'One who is awake' – in the sense of having 'woken up' to Reality. It is therefore not a name but a title, first given to a man called Siddhartha Gautama, who lived 2,500 years ago in northern India. At the age of thirty-five, after years of striving, he gained Enlightenment while in profound meditation. During the remaining forty-five years of his life he walked over much of northern India, spreading his teaching about the way to Enlightenment. This teaching is therefore known in the East as the *Buddha-Dharma* – the 'teaching of the Enlightened One'. Travelling from place to place, the Buddha taught numerous disciples, many of whom also gained Enlightenment. They in turn taught others, and in this way an unbroken chain of teaching has continued, right down to the present day.

The Buddha made no claim to divinity; there is no concept of a creator god in Buddhism. He was a human being who through tremendous efforts transformed himself and transcended the human predicament with its attendant sufferings. The state of Enlightenment which he reached has three main facets. It is a state of wisdom, a total understanding of the true nature of things. It is also a source of infinite compassion, of boundless love for all beings, which expresses itself in the spontaneous desire to help them free themselves from suffering. Lastly, it is the total liberation of all the energies of the psycho-physical organism, so that they are at the service of the fully conscious . mind.

Buddhism sees life as being a process of constant change. This process can be confined to a single 'level', or it can consist of development and evolution. The decisive factor is always our own mind. An ancient Buddhist text begins: 'Our life is shaped by our mind; we become what we think.' Buddhism has developed a number of highly effective methods for working on the mind, methods which allow people to transform themselves positively.

As there is no creator (or judging) god, there is no idea in Buddhism of anyone *having* to be a Buddhist. Buddhism has never, in its 2,500 years, looked for converts with 'fire and sword'. Love and non-violence are essential Buddhist principles. Naturally, Buddhists would say that one can become a happier and better person if one decides to follow the Buddhist path, but Buddhism offers itself as an opportunity: its methods and teachings are available to all those who want to make use of them. People are welcome to take as little or as much of Buddhism as they feel ready for. They may simply practise some meditation to gain peace of mind and relief from psychological difficulties, or they might want to go all the way to Enlightenment.

To become a Buddhist in the full sense means committing oneself to the *Buddha, Dharma,* and *Sangha* – sometimes referred to as the 'Three Jewels'. One centres one's life upon gaining Enlightenment as the Buddha did. To do this one takes advantage of the Dharma – the various teachings and practices of the Buddhist tradition – as tools of self-transformation. One also needs to be in contact with a Sangha – other people who are trying to transform themselves in the same way. Thus one can share experiences, offer mutual help and friendship, and learn from those more advanced than oneself.

Buddhism is a path to freedom. The gate to that path is open to all: men and women, young and old, people of all nationalities, races, and backgrounds.

Buddhism for the West

Despite a few tentative contacts in previous times, Buddhism has become really known in the West only in the last hundred years. Even in the early sixties, when a number of scripture translations and scholarly works were in circulation, there were very few serious practitioners. It was against this background that Sangharakshita founded the Friends of the Western Buddhist Order.

Sangharakshita's name belies his origins. He is English, and was born in London in 1925. He became a Buddhist in his teens, and after the war spent twenty years in India. He was ordained as a Buddhist monk in 1950, and for the next fifteen years stayed in India studying, meditating, teaching, and writing about many aspects of Buddhism. During this time he had contact with exponents of all the main schools of Buddhism, and received initiation and teachings from some of the most respected Tibetan lamas of this century. In 1966 he returned to settle in the West, and founded the FWBO in 1967.

The FWBO has a number of distinctive features, which make it stand out from other attempts to establish Buddhism in the West:

We recognize that new social and cultural conditions may mean doing things in a new way.

Before the arrival of the FWBO, most Buddhist teaching in the West was carried out in line with traditional forms developed in the East. Teachers came from Sri Lanka, Thailand, Burma, or Japan (and more recently from Tibet), and largely tried to transplant their own particular forms of Buddhism wholesale into the Western environment.

The FWBO, however, is committed to presenting Buddhism in a way that is relevant to the modern West. The conditions under which we live have a tremendous effect on us. The modern industrialized environment of skyscrapers, fast cars, television, and computers, is a world away from the conditions under which traditional Buddhism evolved and thrived. It will require some new and different agents to dissolve the psychological and spiritual barriers which keep Westerners from the path to Enlightenment. We have therefore recognized that some of the *forms* through which the central experiences of Buddhism are expressed may need to be adapted to our new circumstances.

At the same time, we have been careful not to 'throw the Buddha out with the bath-water'. The essence of Buddhism is universal and unchanging, and it is that essence that we are trying to communicate. From that point of view, we are a fully 'traditional' Buddhist school.

We derive inspiration from the entire Buddhist tradition.

There were other Buddhist groups in the West before the FWBO. However, nearly all of them were devoted to the study and practice of just one Buddhist school. The view of the FWBO is that Western Buddhists should feel free to draw on the whole Buddhist tradition for inspiration. We are therefore not devoted just to Theravada, to Zen, or to Tibetan Buddhism. Within the FWBO we study and practise whatever we find useful for our development, regardless of which Buddhist tradition it comes from.

We are open to Western art and culture as an aid to personal development.

The FWBO stays faithful to the Buddhist tradition as a whole – it does not mix Buddhism with other religious or spiritual traditions. At the same time, we are prepared to draw on sources of *inspiration* outside Buddhism if they are helpful. In particular, we have devoted time to the exploration of Western art and literature to find artists, poets, and writers whose work reflects some glimmerings of the Dharma. This means that, as Westerners, we do not have to cut loose from our own cultural roots to take up Buddhism; we can appreciate and use what is best in our own culture as a bridge to an understanding of the Dharma.

The FWBO's approach has been very popular. The FWBO now has centres around the world, and is in contact with many thousands of people. One of the greatest surprises about the FWBO's development has been the wide range of its appeal. Its approach has worked not just in Western countries, but in the slums and villages of India.

As well as expanding world-wide, the FWBO has also deep-
ened. In the early days, Sangharakshita taught all the classes,
gave all the lectures, led every course and retreat. Now he has
nearly completed the process of handing over responsibility to
others. A new generation of people – members of the Western
Buddhist Order – will take the FWBO forward. So let's take a
look at the Order that is at the heart of the FWBO.

Sangharakshita

The Western Buddhist Order

The nucleus of the FWBO is the Western Buddhist Order, and it is the members of that Order who are responsible for directing the FWBO's activities. Each local FWBO centre is an independent, autonomous body; what binds it to the others is the link of common practice and friendship between the Order members who work in our centres around the world.

What does it mean to be an Order member?

The members of our Order are people who have fully committed themselves to following the Buddhist Path to Enlightenment. They have made that commitment the central point around which everything else in their lives revolves. In particular, they have committed themselves to Sangharakshita as their spiritual teacher, and to the Western Buddhist Order as the context in which they are trying to gain Enlightenment.

Are Order members monks or nuns?

The Order is open to any man or woman who is sincerely committed to the Buddhist path, not just to those who want to live a monastic life-style. The kind of monasticism found in the Buddhist East is not necessarily relevant or helpful to people living in modern society. Although we try to lead a '100% Buddhist life', members of our Order are not, therefore, monks or nuns.

If they are not monks or nuns, how do Order members live?

One's commitment to Enlightenment can be expressed through any life-style, so long as it is ethical and contains no elements that actively prevent one from developing. Order members live in many different ways. To give an example, in 1995 around our centre in Norwich, there were about two dozen men and women Order members. Some worked full-time running the centre, working on our publications, or in a retail gift business which raises money for the FWBO in the UK and abroad. Those working outside the FWBO included a builder, a writer, a musician, artists, and teachers of yoga, T'ai Chi Chu'an, etc. Several were engaged in teaching Buddhism and meditation. A few lived in families bringing up children, several women had grown-up children at the point of leaving home, and a number lived alone or in single-sex communities or shared homes. All were practising meditation and doing whatever they could to further their development as Buddhists. All were working in some way to offer the riches of the Buddhist tradition to more people.

What rules do Order members have to follow?

There are no rules. Rules have a tendency to hinder rather than help, since they often have the effect of preventing people from thinking for themselves. As Buddhism does not recognize the existence of a creator god, there are no commandments to obey either. At the time of their ordination, all Order members undertake to practise a traditional set of ethical precepts. These point to the basic principles that are to be applied to all actions of body, speech, and mind. With the help of these precepts, Order members try to develop a positive approach in all situations. Men and women Order members take the same precepts, and practise on an equal basis.

How do you become an Order member?

It usually takes several years to become ready for ordination. Ordination is a lifelong commitment, and obviously a very serious step. It is open to anyone to ask for ordination when they feel they want to be ordained. The request is then considered by Sangharakshita or other senior Order members, taking into account the opinions of those Order members who know the person in question well. Nobody is ever refused ordination, but people are sometimes asked to spend more time in preparation. The ordination is performed by a senior Order member known as a Preceptor, usually in the context of a special ordination retreat.

At the time of the ordination ceremony the person being ordained is given a new name. This is usually taken from the Sanskrit or Pali languages. The meaning of the name expresses spiritual qualities which they either already exhibit or which are potential in them. To an Order member, this name is a constant reminder of the spiritual quest to which he or she is committed.

At FWBO classes or other public occasions, Order members usually wear a *kesa*. This is a strip of silk-like material, either white or gold, worn around the neck. It is embroidered with three flaming jewels. These stand for the Buddha, the Dharma, and the Sangha. Most Order members wear a white kesa; a golden-yellow kesa indicates that its wearer has publicly committed himself or herself to leading a celibate life-style.

Some senior members of the Western Buddhist Order, 1995

What the FWBO has to offer

As we have seen, the FWBO was founded in 1967. At first its
growth was slow, but with the years it has expanded, and has
applied the Buddhist vision to more and more areas of life.
Now, in many parts of the world, the FWBO's facilities have
been developed to such an extent that it is possible to live one's
whole life in situations which are conducive to spiritual development. This idea is expressed in what is sometimes referred
to as 'the FWBO mandala'.

A mandala is a symbol of wholeness and balanced development. In essence it is a harmonious arrangement of different
aspects around a central focus – the outer parts being aspects
and expressions of the central point or idea. Here the term
covers all the different ways in which the central vision of the
FWBO might express itself in a particular place. If a team of
Order members has the time and resources to unfold its vision
to the full, then the mandala will probably include a public
centre, several kinds of residential community, some Right
Livelihood businesses, and a network of friendships and personal contacts. These form the four sides of the mandala, and
between them they cover most of what the FWBO has to offer.
We shall look at each of them in turn.

Before we do that, however, we need first to think about what
is at the centre of the FWBO mandala. What is the central focus,
or vision, that underlies our activities? We could put a figure of
the Buddha in the middle, for it is his Enlightenment that
provides the inspiration for the mandala to unfold. Or we could
put the Western Buddhist Order there, for it is Order members
who guide and direct FWBO activities. But perhaps it would be
best simply to put in the centre a vision of personal development. This is, after all, what inspires people to get involved. The
rest of the mandala comes into existence because people have
a vision, or an intuition, that there is more to life, more to
themselves, than they have discovered so far. It is this vision,

together with the practical methods for its realization, that the FWBO has to offer.

Now we have an idea of what lies at the heart of the mandala, let's explore its various aspects.

The Centre

A Buddhist centre is the open door to the mandala, and acts as most people's first point of contact with the FWBO. Our centres offer broad programmes of activities. Here are some brief outlines of the most important:

Meditation

Meditation is the 'royal road' to personal development. It is a direct method of working on the mind in order to transform it. Within the Buddhist tradition there are literally thousands of meditation practices. For a beginner, the sheer wealth of methods can be confusing. However, all these practices fall into two great groups, depending on their main aim.

The first group includes those which calm and refresh the mind. They relax physical tensions and psychological blocks, and leave us in a concentrated, deeply contented state. Most of the time our minds are like water whipped into waves by distractions and the pressures of modern life. As a result, we spend our lives in touch with only the surface of our minds where we are tossed about by the waves. This first group of meditation practices calms things down, so that the waters become clear, and we are left with an 'oceanic' feeling of calm, and even bliss.

The second group of practices aims at developing wisdom. In the Buddhist context this is sometimes called 'Insight into Reality'. These practices enable us to experience our true nature. Through doing this we come to understand our place in the universe: our existential struggles, our concerns about the meaning of life, our fear of death, all come to an end. It is as though, through our practice of calming meditations, we have made the waters of our minds still and clear, and now we can see through the clear water down to the very bottom. It is this seeing into our depths which gives rise to true wisdom.

Within the FWBO we use a number of meditations, drawn from both groups of practices. However, it is not possible to get very far with the second group until you have developed a measure of calm. You'll be wasting your time trying to see to the bottom of your mind if the surface is whipped by the winds of restlessness and distraction. So until they are very experienced in meditation, most people attending FWBO centres are encouraged to concentrate on two practices whose aim is to give peace of mind and produce a positive emotional attitude.

The first practice that most people learn is called the 'Mindfulness of Breathing'. As its name implies, it is a meditation which uses the breath as an object of concentration. It is a particularly good antidote for restlessness and anxiety – an extremely common problem in our times. Concentration on the breath has a positive effect on one's entire physical and mental state. The breath is also portable, which means you can do the practice anywhere! The meditation has four progressive stages, leading to a highly enjoyable level of concentration.

The second practice is called the 'Metta Bhavana'. This translates as 'the development of unlimited friendliness'. It brings about a gentle but radical transformation of our emotional state. Through it we can overcome negative feelings such as fear and dislike, and replace them with a confident, kind, and outwardgoing approach to life. We start the meditation by trying to improve our feelings towards ourselves, and then work in expanding stages, until finally we arrive at a powerful feeling of love for all beings, all forms of life.

Meditation is a subtle process whose benefits multiply over time. The practice of sitting meditation is not an end in itself, however. Gradually, with practice, the positive states which we achieve in meditation spill over into the rest of our life. Eventually, these feelings of calm, friendliness, and clarity will be with us all the time: they will have become the natural way our minds work.

At FWBO centres, meditation instruction is given by experienced Order members, who have themselves been practising meditation for years. Classes and courses are open to everyone: some people want to improve their concentration for work, study, or sports, while others are looking for calm and peace of mind. Then there are people trying to answer fundamental questions about life. With regular practice, meditation can help all of them to find what they are looking for.

Learning about Buddhism

We hope, too, that people will want to learn something about Buddhism. All our centres offer courses, study groups, and series of talks on Buddhism. These range from introductory talks and courses to the more advanced study of Buddhist texts.

Our aim, always, is to do full justice to the Buddhist tradition, while presenting it in a way which is relevant and useful for Westerners.

Sangharakshita is a respected scholar whose works have been influential in both the East and the West. Several more Order members are currently making their mark in the academic world. Even so, Buddhism is something to be practised. The Buddha described his teaching as a raft to carry people away from suffering to the 'further shore' of Enlightenment. When the Dharma brings so much happiness if you actually practise it, there can be little point in a merely academic approach.

For the Dharma to take you to the 'further shore' of Enlightenment, Buddhist tradition says that you must do three things: listen, reflect, and meditate on it. Within the FWBO, chances to *listen* to the Dharma come mainly in the form of talks and lectures by Order members. Since returning to the West, Sangharakshita has given hundreds of talks on Buddhism. (Most of them are available on tape; see 'Finding Out More'.) Over the years a strong tradition of public speaking has also grown up within the Order.

Reflecting on the Dharma can be done individually, but it is often more effective when done with others in a study group. Studying with others gives us the chance to clarify our understanding, share our experience, and learn new approaches. Some Buddhist texts are not very easy to access; a good study group leader will be able to bring a text to life, making it immediate and relevant.

We draw on texts from all aspects of Buddhist tradition. For example, on a typical large retreat there were groups studying the *Udana* (a text from the Pali Canon), *Entering the Path of Enlightenment* (an Indian Mahayana work by Shantideva), and *The Tibetan Book of the Dead*.

Meditating on the Dharma is the third stage. All study retreats and workshops include regular sessions of meditation. We also often use readings of Buddhist texts in a meditative context, letting their meaning sink deeply into our minds.

In these ways people are helped to come to a clear understanding of Buddhism, along with the means of putting it into practice. Whether you just want to find out something about Buddhism, or you are already practising and want further help in 'sailing your raft', our centres will have something to offer.

Developing Body and Mind

Buddhism aims to develop the whole person. This naturally includes the body. Buddhism has never suffered from the idea – which has bedevilled Western philosophy – of a total split between mind and matter. In the West this has led to the body being either devalued, or over-valued in defiant reaction to its being held in such low esteem. Buddhists regard their bodies as the physical vehicles in which they will gain Enlightenment, and thus follow a middle way, neither ill-treating nor glorifying them.

To have the energy to make progress in our personal development, we need to do what we can to maintain our bodies in good condition. Also, though meditation is the direct way of working on the mind, we can positively affect the mind by working with our body. Some of our centres offer classes in physical disciplines such as hatha-yoga, T'ai Chi Ch'uan, and massage.

Teachers of these disciplines at FWBO centres are carefully selected. They are all meditators, capable of bringing an added degree of awareness to a class. They also have a clear understanding of the relationship between body and mind, and treat their disciplines as ways of developing the mind as well as the body.

A number of full-time specialists in these and allied disciplines have come together in East London under the name Bodywise, offering teaching courses in T'ai Chi Ch'uan, hatha-yoga, and Alexander Technique, as well as a wide range of complementary medical treatments such as osteopathy, acupuncture, and shiatsu, not only for Buddhists but for members of the public. Similar centres are being developed in other cities.

Retreats

Many people, perhaps most, begin to discover just what a positive difference Buddhism can make to their lives when they go on retreat. Practising meditation for an evening at a centre is valuable, but it's a very short space of time. When we leave the haven of the centre, all too often we go out into bleak city streets and noisy traffic. Through meditation we have increased our awareness, but now the onslaught of the city environment encourages us to close down the hatches again.

A retreat is a period of time spent in quiet and peaceful surroundings, devoted to meditation and other Buddhist practices. It gives us time and a tranquil environment. We can use it to allow our consciousness to expand, to tune in more deeply to ourselves. It is a chance to shake off the dust of the city and of our old self. In a safe environment, we can discover and explore richer ways of living our lives.

There are many different kinds of FWBO retreat. Some are specifically for beginners, others concentrate on study, others combine meditation with a physical discipline such as yoga or T'ai Chi Ch'uan. The number of different kinds of retreat is as great as the number of spiritual practices. Typically, though, a retreat will have a balanced programme including several periods of meditation, some study and/or talks on Buddhist themes, yoga or other physical disciplines, communication exercises, and puja.

All our centres run regular retreats, and many now have their own country retreat centres. We also have a number of large retreat centres which cater for people from a wide area. Here are brief profiles of the most important of them:

Padmaloka: A large country house in Norfolk, set in six acres of grounds. This is our main UK retreat centre for men. It provides a year-round programme of retreats for men at all levels of involvement with the FWBO, though it specializes in retreats for men who are working towards ordination.

Vajraloka: Our main centre for intensive meditation retreats for men. It was established in the late seventies in converted farm buildings in a quiet valley in North Wales. People come from around the world to spend time here, deepening their meditation practice, and drawing on the great experience of the resident community of meditators.

Vajrakuta: Situated close to Vajraloka, men's study retreats are held here under the guidance of a community of well-qualified study leaders. In addition, the community has taken on responsibility for developing programmes of study in the FWBO as a whole, both at the level of Order members and of those who are interested and involved but not yet members of the Order.

Taraloka: Our main centre for women's retreats. A complex of buildings in gentle countryside in Shropshire, England. Taraloka runs many different kinds of retreat, and is attracting interest among women Buddhists outside the FWBO.

Guhyaloka: 'The Secret Realm', perched high in the mountains of south-eastern Spain. A wild and beautiful 200-acre valley, it is a centre for long retreats during which men are ordained into the Western Buddhist Order.

Tiratanaloka: Set in a beautiful part of South Wales, this is the retreat centre for women training for ordination. The ordination retreats themselves are also held here.

Sadhamma Pradeep and *Hsuan Tsang* are our two principal Indian retreat centres, catering for the massive Indian enthusiasm for retreats. In addition, *Aryaloka* in New Hampshire, USA, *Vijayaloka* in New South Wales, Australia, *Kühhude* near Essen in Germany, and *Tararu* near Auckland, New Zealand, are well-used retreat centres for their respective areas.

Apart from programmed retreats, several of our retreat centres also make provision for people to come and stay for an extended period, living as part of the centre community.

Our retreats for beginners are usually mixed, but more advanced retreats and some of our major retreat centres are for either men or women only.

Single-Sex Activities

In Buddhist tradition it has always been common practice to separate the sexes for more intensive practice of the Dharma. However, when Sangharakshita returned to the West from India, he assumed that this separation was a purely cultural phenomenon. In the early days of the FWBO all our activities were mixed. Then, in the early seventies, we began experimenting with some retreats for men or women only. Most people (often to their own surprise) found them more satisfying. So nowadays all our more advanced retreats (as well as most of our communities and Right Livelihood business teams) are either for men or for women.

There seem to be two main factors which make single-sex situations particularly helpful. The first is that most people are physically attracted to the opposite sex. While that is quite natural, anything which pulls us even subtly towards the world of the senses is a distraction from deep meditation. So both men and women tend to find it easier to explore their inner depths in situations where there are no 'distracting attractions'.

The other factor is that an important aspect of spiritual development is the discovery of psychological wholeness. Both men and women need to develop masculine *and* feminine qualities in order to be truly happy. It is easier to develop the qualities of your other 'polarity' if they are not being supplied for you by having a member of the opposite sex around. Personal development is also about overcoming conditioning and stereotyped views of oneself. Many of these stereotypes are based on gender, and it is easier to go beyond them in an all-male or all-female situation.

Despite hearing all this theory, some people are still a little wary of single-sex activities. Often they have had bad previous experiences in single-sex situations (such as boarding schools). The only real solution is to try out a single-sex retreat with an open mind. The Buddha always encouraged people to rely on their own experience. Come along and decide for yourself.

Devotion and Ritual

Among the practices and activities that our centres offer are a number of devotional rituals. During these, we do things like bow to a statue of the Buddha and chant *mantras* – strings of sound which have no (or very little) intelligible meaning. Some people may wonder how it can be that Buddhism, which is such a clear and rational teaching, should concern itself with such things.

Human beings are not just rational animals. We are all driven at least as much by our emotions as by our intellects. We have unconscious depths, whose magical processes we sometimes glimpse through our dream life. Buddhism is pragmatic; as human beings are not just rational animals, it would be quite irrational to treat them as if they were. Clearly you can't 'win round' all the aspects of a human being by simply addressing the rational faculty: you have to address each aspect in its own language. So we employ colour, beauty, and devotional ritual to involve our emotions in the process of self-transformation. We use visual symbols and sound-symbols (*mantras*) to speak to our unconscious depths.

Although these practices don't work on a rational level, they do have a clear purpose and way of functioning which can be explained. Let's take an example. All FWBO centres have a shrine, decorated with flowers, of which the centrepiece is an image of the Buddha. This is entirely traditional – and was undoubtedly interpreted as 'idol worship' by early Western missionaries to the East. However, no one is worshipping images. The statue of the Buddha is a reminder of the state of Buddhahood which we are trying to attain. Even if we know nothing of Buddhism, a well-sculpted figure of the Buddha can convey a great deal. It sits serene, dignified, calm, and tranquil, in a perfectly balanced position. Without using any words, it can communicate a feeling for the natural dignity which human beings can possess. Contemplating it, something of these qualities rubs off. We come away feeling a little more serene and dignified ourselves.

Buddhist ritual is a 'rational ritual'. Our devotion to the Buddha is in no sense like the worship offered to a creator god. Rather it is a means of developing the qualities of an Enlightened being in ourselves.

There are two main devotional ceremonies (known as pujas) commonly used within the FWBO. The 'Short Puja' deepens our feelings for the Buddha, Dharma, and Sangha, which are the three indispensable means of gaining Enlightenment. The 'Sevenfold Puja' is a longer and more elaborate ritual. Its purpose is to bring about the arising of the *bodhichitta* – an overwhelming feeling of compassion which leads us to follow the path to Enlightenment in order to help all living beings. In these pujas we also use *mantras* – sound-symbols evocative of different aspects of the Enlightenment experience.

Buddhist devotion, especially in a large gathering of people, can be a very rich experience. It gives all the aesthetic satisfaction which we usually associate with an artistic performance.

Festivals

Having found a path which leads to complete happiness, Buddhists have much to celebrate. Festivals form an important part of our calendar. Some are celebrated at individual FWBO centres; others on a national basis. Here is a list of our main festivals:

15 February. Parinirvana Day: The commemoration of the Buddha's death. Also on this day we remember friends and relatives who died during the past twelve months. Because of the profound Buddhist understanding of death, this isn't a mournful or gloomy day. It can be very moving and beautiful.

6 April. FWBO Day: The anniversary of the founding of the FWBO in 1967.

7 April. WBO Day: The anniversary of the founding of the Western Buddhist Order, one year later.

8 April. The Buddha's Birthday: Marking the Buddha's birth at Kapilavastu in present-day Nepal.

April/May. Buddha Day (Wesak): The most important festival of the Buddhist year. It celebrates the Buddha's attainment of Enlightenment.

June/July. Dharma Day: The Buddha first communicated his discovery of the path to Enlightenment in the Deer Park at

Sarnath. Dharma Day celebrates the Buddha's teaching, and our own good fortune in being able to follow it.

August. Padmasambhava Day: Padmasambhava was the Indian teacher who was instrumental in establishing Buddhism in Tibet. He is the central figure of the Nyingma School of Tibetan Buddhism. It was this school to which most of Sangharakshita's Tibetan teachers belonged.

October/November. Sangha Day: The Sangha is the community of followers of the Buddha. This day is a chance to celebrate the fact that we are not alone, totally reliant on our own resources for our development.

Where dates are not given exactly, it is because the festival is celebrated on a full moon day, or some other day fixed by the lunar calendar, so dates vary from year to year. Sometimes festivals are celebrated on a weekend close to the actual date. All festivals except WBO Day are open to everybody.

Exploring the Arts

As we saw in an earlier section, the FWBO is trying to build bridges between traditional Buddhism and Western culture. For us as Westerners our art and culture is very important; we are rooted in it. It is almost impossible for us to abandon it in favour of a Buddhist culture which is couched in Eastern terms. So, through some of our activities, we are attempting to initiate a dialogue. Our perspective as Buddhists means that we have a standpoint from which to develop a consistent critique of Western art. At the same time, some of the greatest Western artists, poets, and writers have had intuitions of the higher states to which Buddhist practice leads.

We hope that, eventually, out of this dialogue a marriage will develop. Inspired by the Dharma, Western artists, composers, sculptors, poets, and dramatists may take our culture to new heights. This is by no means a fanciful idea. The Renaissance in Europe was sparked off by the discovery of Classical Greek art and thought. Now, in Buddhism, the West is coming into contact with an even more sublime product of the human spirit. We can expect something very special to take place.

The FWBO already numbers within its ranks a good number of working artists, musicians, and writers. Some of our artists are producing traditional Buddhist images, which are gradually becoming more Western in appearance and 'feel'; others are working within the Western tradition. In the UK we have a busy Arts Centre in London (as well as one in Brighton), which provides space for artists to work, puts on lectures, exhibitions, and recitals of music and poetry, and affords facilities for people who live locally as well as for those more closely connected with the FWBO to practise and enhance their appreciation of the arts in all their forms. In India the Ashvaghosha Project takes the Dharma to the people of the villages by way of street drama and story-telling.

We feel confident that our exploration of the arts will enrich our Buddhist practice, and that our contact with Buddhism will give us an even more profound understanding of the potential – and limitations – of Western culture.

Deepening Communication

To be in real communication with other human beings is vital, not just for our higher spiritual development, but also for our everyday happiness. At our centres, and sometimes on retreats, we hold sessions of 'communication exercises' to practise deep and open communication.

Sangharakshita found these exercises being used in India by someone training teachers in communication skills. Once one has overcome some initial feeling of strangeness, they can be hugely enjoyable. Their effects include the release of emotional energy and making strong connections with other people in record time!

All these many activities make FWBO centres lively places. Also, years of meditation classes build up a tangible atmosphere, which can help newcomers to develop meditative states of mind. We try to make our centres attractive and aesthetically pleasing, so that the whole environment serves as a support for what we are trying to do.

A public centre is most people's way in to the FWBO. They come interested in meditation or yoga, Buddhism or the arts. Often that initial interest spills over as they start to see how the centre's activities are interrelated and mutually supportive to higher states of consciousness. Now that we have entered the FWBO mandala, it is time to explore its other sides.

Living in Communities

You have been going along regularly to an FWBO centre. You are trying to lead a more aware life. You have gone from meditating once a week at the centre to meditating regularly at home. Tonight you fancy doing a short period of meditation before going to bed. Just as you sit down the crash of the front door announces that one of your flat-mates is back from an evening out. The TV goes on (loud) in the room next door. You do your best to ignore it and sink into the calm of meditation. After a while there is a knock on your door. In bursts your *other* flat-mate. 'Oh! You were meditating? Sorry.' He is excited because he wants to tell you that he's just bought a drum kit....

It was this sort of experience which led to our first residential communities.

Experiments in community living began in the early days of the FWBO. Over the years we have gained a great deal of experience of what makes a community successful. Today we have a large number of communities around the world. They range in size from three to about two dozen people. They also vary in their living arrangements. Some communities comprise a few friends living together in a house or flat, usually near a centre. They eat together but otherwise live relatively separate lives. Nonetheless, they enjoy the advantage of living with congenial people who share their interests. At the other end of the scale are more intensive situations where everyone actively practises together, with a programme of regular meditation, study, and community meetings. All these more intensive communities, like our retreats, are for men or women only, though some make provision for entertaining guests of the opposite sex.

Communities offer a supportive environment for spiritual practice, and the chance to deepen friendships with others who share our interests. A further benefit of community life is the chance to live with people who are more advanced on the Buddhist path than ourselves. Observing them at close quarters, we can learn a great deal from how they live their lives. People can also get to know each other better. That means they can be more useful in exchanging advice on how to resolve problems or take one's development further.

It can also be extremely supportive to have others around who are meditating regularly. In the early stages of spiritual development, our enthusiasm inevitably comes and goes. If we are on our own it is hard to keep self-motivated. It is much easier if we are in daily contact with people whose enthusiasm can feed us.

For many people, joining a community is a decisive turning point. It often represents the step from an interest in Buddhism to a deeper involvement. The more intensive communities can be exciting and challenging, as people inspire one another to take further all aspects of their development. It is often in these communities that new breakthroughs are made. They are thus a sort of leading edge, taking the FWBO to deeper levels of practice and inspiration.

If you would like to explore community life for yourself, Order members at centres can advise you of possible openings in existing communities, or put you in touch with people interested in starting a new one. Most of our communities will take guests for short stays, which will give you an idea of community life. If you like what you see, and don't want to live with a drum kit, the next step is obvious....

Right Livelihood – A New Approach to Working

Right Livelihood is the traditional Buddhist term for work which is ethical and helpful to one's spiritual development. Most of us spend a good deal of our lives working. The work we do has a strong effect on our minds. This is so much the case that we often describe, or even define, people in terms of their work ('he's a stockbroker', 'she's a teacher'). If we do work that is boring or repetitive, ethically dubious, or in an ugly and noisy environment, it will inevitably have a corrosive effect on our minds.

Understanding the large conditioning effect – for better or worse – that work has on us, the FWBO began experimenting with what we call Right Livelihood businesses. We have now set up a large number of work situations which aim at benefiting the people who work in them, and which provide some useful service to society. All these businesses have four aims (though they may vary in the emphasis they place on each of them):

To provide a work situation which helps people to develop as individuals

Most people don't choose their workmates, and often have very little in common with them – beyond a shared dislike of the work they have to do! In the seventies people in the FWBO started setting up situations where they could work together. They wanted to create working environments which were friendly and enjoyable. They approached the whole work experience as a practice which could help their personal development and reinforce their meditation. They used work as a training ground for developing awareness and the capacity to co-operate. They encouraged one another to learn to take initiative and personal responsibility. They found working in this way difficult and challenging, but also very rewarding.

In our Right Livelihood businesses we try, as far as possible, to work co-operatively. There is no power structure of the 'I'm the boss: you do what I say with no questions asked' variety. Most of our businesses are team-based, with each team member being encouraged to take as much responsibility as he or she can. At the same time, in decision-making the voices of those with the greatest spiritual or practical experience will naturally carry the most weight.

To offer something useful to society

Our Right Livelihood businesses aim at benefiting the society with which they interact. Some of them are indirect ways of making a statement of our Buddhist principles. Our vegetarian restaurants are a good example of this. Without overt propagandizing, they make a point about non-violence to animals. Some of our businesses take aspects of Buddhism to people who would never dream of coming to a Buddhist centre. For example, some people are teaching meditation to businessmen, as part of their work as stress management consultants. Moreover, the way the businesses are run communicates Buddhist values to people coming in contact with them and shows what real live Buddhists are like.

Businesses set up by the FWBO have included wholefood shops, vegetarian restaurants, gardening and landscaping, publishing, book-selling, building. An expanding activity is Bodywise, which was described earlier. The biggest business is now Windhorse Trading, which markets gifts, furniture, and decorative objects through (at present) fourteen retail outlets under the name Evolution, and also through independent shops. It has a current annual turnover of over £4,500,000 and employs over a hundred people. All these businesses provide something worthwhile, in ways that do no damage to the environment.

To provide a reasonable level of support for their workers

If you work in one of our businesses you won't end up driving a Porsche. The benefits of working in Right Livelihood are not primarily financial. The businesses give people enough to live on, to meet their need for a reasonable standard of living, dependent on their personal circumstances and needs; for example, a parent will receive more than a single person living in a community. Most of them provide six weeks' paid retreat time a year for each worker as well.

To make a profit to donate to a worthwhile cause

While some profits need to be retained for future expansion, our businesses also try to make a surplus to give away. Over the years our businesses have given away hundreds of thousands of pounds – to help Indian slum-dwellers, children of Tibetan refugees, and to other individuals in need. Some of our businesses are set up in order to finance their local FWBO centres, or to seed new FWBO projects. Windhorse Trading alone provided £200,000 during 1994. Among the projects financed have been translations of Buddhist books into other languages, e.g. Russian; the purchase of land at Bodh-gaya (the site of the Buddha's Enlightenment in India) for the establishment of a vihara or residential centre; and support for the editing and publication of Sangharakshita's lecture and seminar material.

Right Livelihood hasn't been easy. Some of our earlier attempts have fallen by the wayside. Many of our businesses were started with more idealism than money, more willingness than expertise. But we are confident that we know now how to create working situations which can be both personally satisfying and competitive in the business world.

Friendship

In a conversation with Ananda, his attendant and constant companion, the Buddha said that friendship is 'the whole of the spiritual life'. This is a teaching which we take very seriously indeed. By using communication exercises and meditations like the Metta Bhavana, we work to develop an open outward-going interest in other people. We also encourage people to build deep friendships. This emphasis that we place on friendship is quite possibly one of the most important things we have to offer. This is especially so when so many people nowadays lack deep friendships. Increased mobility cuts many of us off from old friends and our wider family. Male friendship, in particular, has suffered a strong decline in recent years. In an increasingly competitive world, many men don't feel able to let down their guard with one another. More and more, we live in small family units, with no significant outside friendships. This is not a healthy situation.

Friendship is a human necessity. It is also a spiritual practice. To make a deep friendship with another human being involves going beyond our own concerns and self-interest to meet them half-way. In particular, if the friendship is with someone more aware and emotionally positive than ourselves, then we can gain tremendously from the experience. In open communication with them we can be lifted on to their level.

This aspect of friendship – friendship with people more advanced than ourselves – is a central part of what we call the Mitra system. 'Mitra' is an ancient Indian word for 'friend'. In this context, a Mitra is someone who is actively involved in the FWBO, and intends to be involved for the foreseeable future. Some Mitras are thinking of one day becoming Order members. Others may remain Mitras indefinitely. Becoming a Mitra marks a deepening of one's involvement with the Order. There are special activities for Mitras, including retreats and study groups. A three-year study course has been designed especially for Mitras who want to gain a good basic understanding of Buddhism.

It is open to anyone to ask to become a Mitra. However, before doing so it is important to understand what it means. In asking to become a Mitra you are, in effect, saying four things:

(1) You have decided that, of all the many Buddhist and other spiritual groups, the FWBO is the one you're going to stay with. At the beginning of your spiritual development it can be useful to try out different things. However, to get very far you need to choose one approach that suits you, and work with that. It's like learning to play tennis. You can try out different ways of playing the shots, but to develop your game you need to stay with one style. If you keep chopping and changing you will never become any good. The same principle holds true for meditation and spiritual development. So a Mitra is someone who has finished shopping around and has decided to practise the Dharma within the context of the FWBO.

(2) You are meditating regularly. Meditation is such an effective means of changing yourself that we naturally expect someone who is beginning to take their development more seriously to meditate regularly.

(3) You are prepared to do what you can to help out. It may be making the tea at a meditation class, helping with publicity, or giving financial support. As a Mitra you really feel that an FWBO centre is *your* centre. So you do what you can to help it, and to support Order members in their work.

(4) You are going to keep in contact with Order members. This is where friendship comes in. Within the FWBO we recognize

that you can't just spray meditation and Buddhism around. Buddhism is a matter of personal experience (which is why you can't get very far by just learning from books). People are unique, and everyone's pattern of development is slightly different. So there is no substitute for personal contact with people who are more experienced than you. They have to get to know you before they can be fully effective in helping you to develop. So when you become a Mitra, you commit yourself to keeping in regular contact with Order members. Usually, from this regular contact, friendships blossom.

Becoming a Mitra isn't automatic. Your request is discussed by Order members, since in accepting your request the Order is also making a commitment. We are committing ourselves to keeping in contact with you and making sure that you have everything you need to develop spiritually.

Once your request is accepted you then take part in a simple ceremony and from then on you are a Mitra. This is acknowledged not only by your local centre but by all Order members. Wherever you go throughout the world, at all our centres, you will be acknowledged as a Mitra, and Mitra activities will be open to you wherever you are.

We have spent time looking at the Mitra system for two reasons. Firstly, it is an example of how we emphasize personal contact. Also, becoming a Mitra is a step which many people want to take after they have explored the FWBO mandala and like what they see.

However, although we have looked at the Mitra system, one of the most important functions of this fourth side of the mandala is to show that the FWBO is not just a system, or a collection of techniques. The FWBO is essentially a constantly enlarging community of people who are practising the Dharma together, helping each other along in every way they can, and co-operating to create the conditions they need for their spiritual development. It is important that we do not lose sight of that fact.

We believe that the FWBO mandala adds up to an excellent setting within which men and women can live increasingly happy and fulfilling lives.

We also have a vision of the mandala expanding, so that more and more aspects of society are positively influenced by it. We are not interested in making the mandala an ivory tower cut off from the world. In fact, our meditation makes us feel an increasing concern for the environment and for our fellow human beings. Two charities that we have established to fund medical and educational work give some indication of this. The Karuna Trust (originally 'Aid For India'), has an ongoing fund-raising programme carried out mainly by gathering pledges from door to door. The money raised goes to support work done in India through its sister organization there, Bahujan Hitay, promoting social development programmes with the ex-Untouchable communities. These include educational, health, and job training projects. To date Karuna has raised some £5,000,000 towards this work. Karuna also separately supports Buddhist activities for the many ex-Untouchables who converted to Buddhism; these include retreat centres and Buddhist classes. ('Karuna' means 'compassion'.)

It may seem an impossible task to turn our current society into one based on love and awareness, which supports people in their efforts to develop towards Enlightenment. However, that is the goal we have in mind. For the time being, we just keep trying to expand the mandala to include more people. Time will tell if our vision can be brought into existence. Whatever happens, it is deeply satisfying for us to watch the mandala expand, and to see people using its facilities to become happier and freer.

Meditators at the London Buddhist Centre

How the FWBO is run

We have now explored the FWBO mandala, and seen what it has to offer. This section gives brief answers to a few more things you might like to know about the FWBO.

How do I become a 'Friend'?

The FWBO is not an organization that you join by paying a subscription. Anyone who comes along to our activities, or who takes an active interest in what we are doing, we describe as a Friend (capital F). Some of our Friends are very actively involved, and attend many classes, etc. Others just come along very occasionally to a talk or festival. Being a Friend puts you under no obligation. We are happy for people to take as much or as little of what we have to offer as feels right to them. At the same time the opportunity of becoming more involved is always there.

How are FWBO centres run?

Each centre is separate, and responsible for running its own affairs. In Britain and most other countries our centres are registered charities. Each centre is run by a council of members of the Western Buddhist Order. They are responsible for looking after all aspects of their centre's classes and administration. One unusual thing about our councils is that we don't decide on things by voting. We work by consensus, talking things through until we come to a general agreement.

What is the relationship between different FWBO centres?

We've seen that each centre is a separate unit. In fact, each FWBO centre has its own flavour and its own particular strengths. However, wherever you go throughout the world, an FWBO centre still feels like an FWBO centre. You may usually go to a centre in London, but if you travel to Helsinki or Auckland, you will still feel quite at home. This is because all our centres are linked by the threads of friendship, common commitment, and practice which unite the Order members who run our centres.

How do you finance things?

We have three main ways of raising funds for our centres. The first is, as we have seen, through our Right Livelihood businesses. Secondly, through charging for classes and retreats. This helps pay our running costs. However, we try to keep our charges quite low, and we give reduced rates for those on low incomes. We are more concerned that people should be able to come along than about making money from them. Our third source of finance is donations. Over the years many people have been very generous in helping us. However, we don't have any wealthy backers or patrons. Lack of money is still a major limitation to our capacity to go out and teach the Dharma to more people in more places.

Finding out more and taking things further

If you have made contact with the FWBO, and you like what you have seen, there are many ways in which you can get more involved. In fact, you can take things further in any of the four areas of the FWBO mandala.

For most people, an FWBO centre will be the first place to explore. Each centre runs a graded series of classes, courses, and events. So you can steadily deepen your understanding and experience of meditation and Buddhism, usually moving from a beginners' meditation class to an introductory course on Buddhism, and from there to a class for regular Friends. Always you'll be allowed to go at your own pace.

When you first come in contact with the FWBO, you tend to associate it pretty much with the Order members and other people at your own local centre. However, as we've seen, the FWBO is a world-wide network of people. Each centre is really unique. So it's good to put your toe in the water of the wider FWBO, to see other Order members, and meet people from different centres. If you live in Britain, one very good way of doing this is to attend weekend or week-long retreats run regularly at major retreat centres such as Taraloka (for women) or Padmaloka (for men), or at local retreat centres such as Rivendell or Water Hall. On these occasions, people come together for meditation, talks by Order members, and study of Buddhist texts.

Another way of keeping in touch with the wider world of the FWBO has been through reading *Dharma Life*, a Buddhist magazine of broad appeal reflecting the values of the FWBO and Sangharakshita's perspective on the Buddhist tradition. It is available from our centres or on subscription. Other periodicals now appearing within the FWBO are: *Lotus Realm*, a magazine by and for women; *Urthona*, an arts magazine; and the *Western*

Buddhist Review, a forum for the in-depth study of particular Buddhist topics.

As well as periodicals, there are now in print a great many books and booklets by Sangharakshita and other Order members, ranging across many aspects of the theory and practice of Buddhism. All our centres have bookstalls where these and other books on Buddhism can be bought. On the subject of publications, if you want a much fuller introduction to the FWBO than this booklet can provide, then *Buddhism For Today* by Alex Kennedy (Subhuti) will give you a complete picture of the FWBO and its underlying principles.

Two other ways of learning more about Buddhism and the FWBO are through cassette tapes and videos. We have a library of hundreds of taped talks on the Dharma by Sangharakshita and other speakers. All these can be bought from Dharmachakra Tapes, who will send you a full catalogue on request. Most centres also run a tape library from which you can borrow most of Sangharakshita's lectures.

As videos have become more and more popular, we have set up Clear Vision, which has produced a series of newsreels showing how the FWBO is developing all over the world, together with videos of television interviews given by Sangharakshita and other FWBO events. These are available to buy or to rent.

The FWBO is expanding throughout the world. Besides sixteen well-established centres and a number of local groups in Great Britain, there are centres in Ireland, Spain, the Netherlands, Germany, Sweden, and Finland, two each in Australia and New Zealand, three (so far!) in the United States, and one in Venezuela – as well as a large and growing presence in western India and a contact point during the winter months in Kathmandu. The situation is changing all the time.

If you don't live within easy reach of a centre, you can write for information to the one nearest you, or to FWBO Central. This office is also the place to write to if you are part of a group or organization wanting to make contact with the FWBO.

The FWBO Communications Office has been set up as a resource for the media. It provides reliable information on all aspects of Buddhism, as well as informed comment on current affairs from a Buddhist point of view.

We hope this booklet has given you a picture of the FWBO and what we are trying to do. We offer a way of personal development tried and tested over the last 2,500 years, in a form readily accessible to people living in a world of computers and nuclear power. Entering the FWBO mandala means starting out on a journey of self-discovery and self-transformation. We offer our facilities equally to people who are just looking to become a little happier and calmer in their lives, and to spiritual adventurers who want to journey to Enlightenment. The FWBO is an opportunity. You can always take things further, but at your own pace. Whether you just want to explore a side of the mandala or leap into its centre, you will be made very welcome.